D0688952

We
Shall
Overcome

The Freedom Riders

Rachel Tisdale

PowerKiDS
press.

New York

Published in 2014 by The Rosen Publishing Group
29 East 21st Street, New York, NY 10010

Produced for Rosen by Calcium Creative Ltd
Editor for Calcium Creative Ltd: Sarah Eason
US Editor: Joshua Shadowens
Designer: Paul Myerscough

Photo credits: Cover: Birmingham Civil Rights Institute (bg), Getty Images: Paul
Schutzer/Time Life Pictures(fg). Inside: Corbis: Bettmann 14, 16–17, 20; Getty
Images: Lee Lockwood/Time Life Pictures 21, Paul Schutzer/Time & Life Pictures
13, 22; Library of Congress: Walter Albertin 7, Esther Bubley, FSA/OWI 1, 9, Orlando
Fernandez 27, Carol M. Highsmith Archive 10, 25, Lewis W. Hine 5, Warren K. Leffler
24, Thoma J. O'Halloran 26, Marion S. Trikosko 3, 19, US Navy photo 18, Marion
Post Walcott, OWI 4, Stanley Wolfson 11; Shutterstock: Bikeriderlondon 29, Brandon
Bourdages 6, Maximus256 12, Pio3 8; Wikimedia Commons: John Morse 28.

Library of Congress Cataloging-in-Publication Data

Tisdale, Rachel.
 The Freedom Riders / by Rachel Tisdale.
    pages cm. — (We shall overcome)
 Includes index.
 ISBN 978-1-4777-6061-1 (library) — ISBN 978-1-4777-6062-8 (pbk.) —
 ISBN 978-1-4777-6063-5 (6-pack)
 1. African American civil rights workers—Biography—Juvenile literature. 2. Civil
rights workers—United States—Biography—Juvenile literature. 3. African
Americans—Civil rights—Southern States—History—20th century—Juvenile
literature. 4. Civil rights movements—Southern States—History—20th century—
Juvenile literature. 5. Southern States—Race relations—Juvenile literature.
 I. Title.
 E185.96.T58 2014
 323.092'2—dc23
 [B]
                                    2013024408

Manufactured in the United States of America

CPSIA Compliance Information: Batch #W14PK5: For Further Information contact Rosen Publishing, New York, New York at 1-800-237-9932

Contents

A Divided Country

For almost 250 years in America, African Americans had been forced into slavery. However, after the Civil War of 1861 to 1865, slavery became illegal. Changes to the law stated that African Americans were now able to move freely within white communities. This enormous change to American society concerned white southerners, most of whom wished to continue living lives that were separate from those of African Americans.

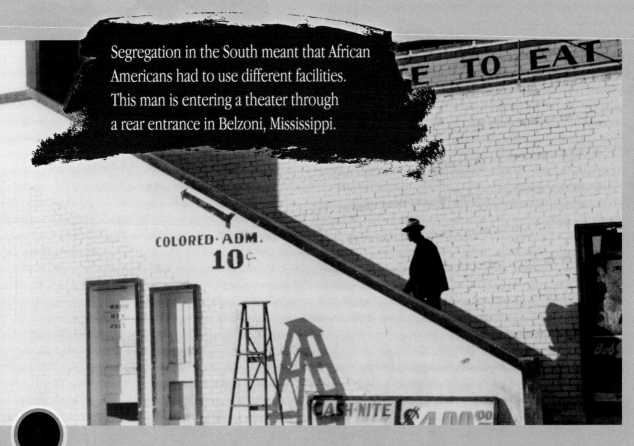

Segregation in the South meant that African Americans had to use different facilities. This man is entering a theater through a rear entrance in Belzoni, Mississippi.

COLORED·ADM.
10¢

WHITE MEN ONLY

CASH NITE

Legally Separate

To maintain separation, white Americans in southern states introduced laws that ensured African Americans and white Americans were separated in most areas of daily life. The laws became known as Jim Crow laws, and the separation of white and African Americans was known as segregation.

Schools for African Americans only, such as this one in Henderson County, Kentucky, were often in poor condition.

Fighting Back

Determined to fight segregation, many African Americans protested against the laws. African American groups gathered together to organize ways in which they could protest against their treatment. Eventually, these groups of protesters grew into an organization called the National Association for the Advancement of Colored People (NAACP).

The Rules

Under segregation, African Americans were unable to vote or attend the same schools as white Americans. African Americans also had to sit separately in restaurants, on public transport, and were made to give up their seats to any white Americans.

The First Protest

In 1944, an important stand was made against the laws on an American public transport bus. An African American woman named Irene Morgan caught a bus from Virginia to Baltimore, Maryland. When Irene was asked to sit at the back of the bus, as Virginia law stated she must, she refused. Irene argued that she was taking a bus that passed between different states, and therefore Virginia law did not apply. However, she was arrested and fined for refusing to move.

To Court

The NAACP took up Irene's case with the US Supreme Court. The Court ruled that the Virginia law was illegal when applied to interstate travelers.

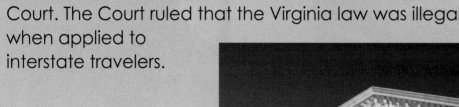

In the Irene Morgan case, the US Supreme Court ruled that it was not right that passengers had to sit in segregated seats when they were traveling between states.

Testing the Law

In 1947, 16 white and African Americans decided to test that the Supreme Court's ruling was being upheld, by traveling on public transport buses between some states in the South. The group were all members of a civil rights organization called the Congress of Racial Equality (CORE). Their interstate bus ride was called the Journey of Reconciliation.

James Farmer was a prominent civil rights campaigner who helped to found the CORE organization in 1942.

CORE Rights

James Farmer was one of a group of people who founded CORE in 1942. The aim of the organization was to use nonviolent protest to gain equal rights for African Americans. Farmer was an African American who had been inspired to help form the protest group because of his own experiences of segregation at school and in public places, such as cinemas. James Farmer was determined to change American society, and he went on to become director of CORE in 1961.

Journey of Reconciliation

For two weeks, the 16 CORE members traveled on public transport between the states of Virginia, Kentucky, North Carolina, and Tennessee. These northernmost states were the least dangerous for African American passengers. During the journey, the CORE members defied the usual segregated seating arrangements. The African Americans sat at the front of the bus, and the white members sat at the back.

"We were filled with vim and vigor, and we hoped that a mass movement could develop…The things we did in the 1940s were the same things that ushered the civil rights revolution." George Houser, one of the 16 CORE members who took part in the 1947 Journey of Reconciliation.

Arrests and Attention

As the journey progressed, the CORE members were arrested and put in jail. The journey soon attracted newspaper attention, and word of the protest spread.

Today, African and white Americans sit side by side on public transport. However, in 1947, this was one of the methods used by CORE members to test segregation.

A Long Journey

The journey was the start of a long civil rights campaign by the CORE organization, and inspired other African Americans to make a stand against segregation on public transport.

Passengers wait to board buses in Louisville, Kentucky. CORE members tested the new rules on interstate travel in the Journey of Reconciliation in 1947.

Riding for Freedom

The 16 CORE members who traveled on the Journey of Reconciliation bus were Ernest Bromley, Igal Roodenko, George Houser, Bayard Rustin, James Peck, Joseph Felmet, Nathan Wright, Conrad Lynn, Wallace Nelson, Andrew Johnson, Eugene Stanley, Dennis Banks, William Worthy, Louis Adams, Worth Randle, and Homer Jack. Some of these brave men would also go on to take part in the Freedom Rides of 1961.

Journeys to Freedom

In 1955, a woman named Rosa Parks challenged segregation on public buses in her home city of Montgomery, Alabama. Rosa was asked to give up her seat for a white passenger on the bus, but when she refused she was arrested and sent to jail. Her actions resulted in a boycott of Montgomery's buses, and many people in the city refused to travel on them for more than a year. In 1956, the US Supreme Court ruled that segregated seating on public transport was illegal.

Further Desegregation

In late 1960, the US Supreme Court passed another law regarding segregation in interstate travel. The Court ordered that restaurants and restrooms at rail stations for interstate passengers should no longer be segregated.

This is the bus stop where, in 1955, Rosa Parks caught the bus on which she refused to give up her seat to a white passenger.

Testing the Law Again

Just as the organization had tested the public transport desegregation law in 1947, CORE decided to also test the Supreme Court's ruling of 1960. The leaders of CORE asked its members to apply to take part in what they called a "Freedom Ride."

The Freedom Route

The volunteers were asked to ride on public transport buses throughout the southern states of Virginia, North and South Carolina, and Georgia, to test segregation once more. Finally, the ride would travel through the southern states of Alabama and Mississippi, ending in New Orleans, Louisiana, on May 17.

The Freedom Riders

In total, 13 CORE members agreed to take part in the 13-day Freedom Ride. The riders understood they would spend time in jail if they were arrested, and that they would face danger from white Americans against desegregation. Some of the riders even wrote wills. They did not expect to return from the journey alive. The group included James Peck, one of the members of the Journey of Reconciliation in 1947.

James Farmer and the CORE organization decided to test the new laws at bus terminals and arranged "Freedom Rides."

The First Bus Leaves

On May 4, 1961, the group of 13 Freedom Riders nervously took their places on the Freedom Ride bus. The bus made its way through Virginia and North Carolina with little trouble. When the bus stopped at terminals, the white Freedom Riders used the "colored" restrooms, and the African Americans used the "white" restrooms.

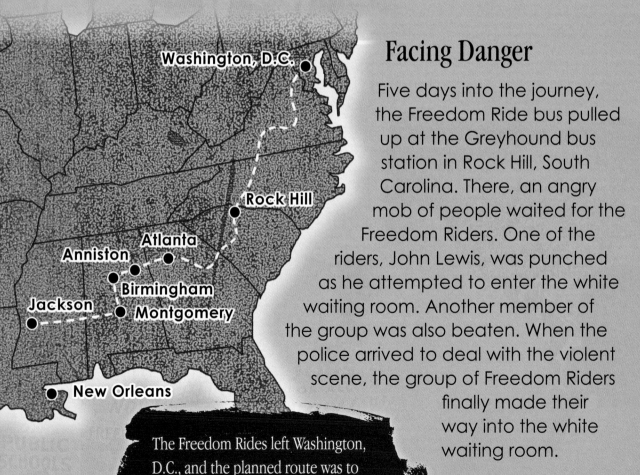

Facing Danger

Five days into the journey, the Freedom Ride bus pulled up at the Greyhound bus station in Rock Hill, South Carolina. There, an angry mob of people waited for the Freedom Riders. One of the riders, John Lewis, was punched as he attempted to enter the white waiting room. Another member of the group was also beaten. When the police arrived to deal with the violent scene, the group of Freedom Riders finally made their way into the white waiting room.

The Freedom Rides left Washington, D.C., and the planned route was to travel all the way to New Orleans.

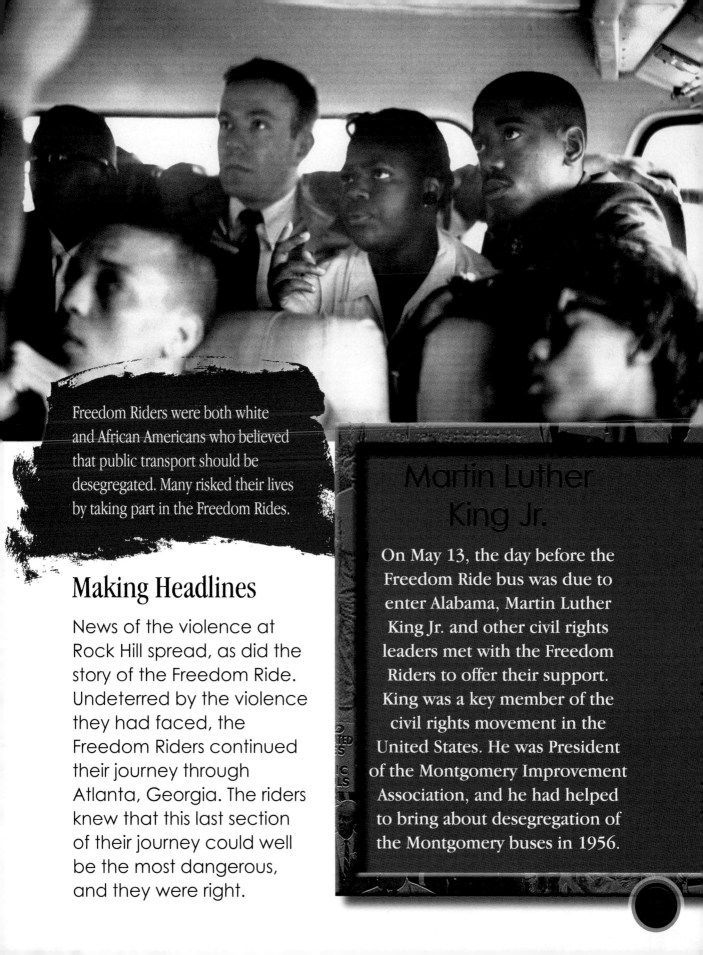

Freedom Riders were both white and African Americans who believed that public transport should be desegregated. Many risked their lives by taking part in the Freedom Rides.

Making Headlines

News of the violence at Rock Hill spread, as did the story of the Freedom Ride. Undeterred by the violence they had faced, the Freedom Riders continued their journey through Atlanta, Georgia. The riders knew that this last section of their journey could well be the most dangerous, and they were right.

Martin Luther King Jr.

On May 13, the day before the Freedom Ride bus was due to enter Alabama, Martin Luther King Jr. and other civil rights leaders met with the Freedom Riders to offer their support. King was a key member of the civil rights movement in the United States. He was President of the Montgomery Improvement Association, and he had helped to bring about desegregation of the Montgomery buses in 1956.

Attacks in Alabama

Before entering Alabama, the Freedom Riders split into two groups. They did this to ensure that they traveled on buses owned by two separate bus companies. In this way they could more fully test the system of segregation being upheld on American public transport. One group of Freedom Riders traveled on a Greyhound company bus and the other group on a Trailways company bus.

Freedom Riders on the Greyhound bus were attacked when the bus entered Anniston, Alabama. The bus was set on fire and the Freedom Riders had to escape.

Police Support

Shockingly, Alabama police, with the support of Alabama state officials, helped the mob's attacks against the Freedom Riders. Police deliberately stayed away from the terminals when the Freedom Ride buses were due to arrive. Heads of the police force in Alabama assured mob members that they would have 15 minutes within which to attack the Freedom Riders before any police attended the scene.

The First Assault

As the Greyhound bus entered Anniston, it was met by a large, angry mob made up of more than 100 people. The crowd quickly surrounded the bus, slashed its tires, and set the bus on fire. Luckily, all of the Freedom Riders managed to get off the bus safely, but they then faced the angry crowd.

Terrible Beatings

When the Trailways bus arrived in Anniston, some of the mob members boarded it, and beat the African American riders who were sitting in the front of the bus. The mob dragged them to the back of the bus where they hit them with bottles and clubs. Many Freedom Riders were badly beaten and left semiconscious at the back of the bus.

> "The people of Alabama are so enraged that I cannot guarantee protection for this bunch of rabble-rousers."
> James Patterson, Governor of Alabama.

Beatings in Birmingham

When the Freedom Ride buses arrived in Birmingham, Alabama, they were again met by an angry mob. Armed with iron bars, the mob then battered the protesters until many of them were beaten unconscious and hospitalized.

You Can't Ride

Despite the violence they had faced, the Riders who had not been badly injured decided to continue with their journey. The day after the mob attack, they tried to board a bus to Montgomery. However, no bus would take them. The bus companies feared further damage to their buses, and the bus drivers feared for their lives. Their bus journey had come to an end. The Freedom Riders flew to New Orleans. The first Freedom Ride had ended, but the protest had not.

Diane Nash

Diane Nash was one of the founding members of the Student Nonviolent Coordinating Committee (SNCC), a group of students who were determined to campaign for civil rights. Diane coordinated and helped to organize the Freedom Rides from her base in Nashville, Tennessee. It was Diane's job to recruit new riders, speak to the press, and gain the support of national leaders and the government. It was in part due to Diane's unswerving support that the Freedom Riders attempted to continue with their rides after the terrible violence they experienced in Birmingham.

"Violence needs to be addressed. I think the civil rights movement has demonstrated how to resolve human conflicts." Diane Nash.

James Peck was severely beaten when the Freedom Ride entered Birmingham, Alabama. Here, he takes part in a picket at the Trailways bus station in New York after the first Freedom Ride was forced to an end.

On to Montgomery

Violence had forced the first Freedom Ride to end early. However, the Freedom Riders were determined to continue with their protest. The riders met in Nashville. They made plans to travel to Birmingham and Montgomery, then on to Mississippi and New Orleans. Some members of the first Freedom Ride, including John Lewis, agreed to take part in the second ride, too.

Presidential Protection

The violence in Alabama had made the national news, and had come to the attention of President John F. Kennedy. The president was concerned that the second group of Freedom Riders would meet with the same violence that the first group had faced. To ensure their safety, Kennedy arranged for a police helicopter to escort and protect the Freedom Riders on their journey between Birmingham and Montgomery.

President John F. Kennedy sent police to escort the Freedom Riders safely into Montgomery, Alabama.

John Lewis was one of the Freedom Riders who was badly beaten in Montgomery.

Mob Attack

Police escort had kept the Freedom Riders safe during their journey to Montgomery. However, police protection ended there. In readiness for the arrival of the Freedom Riders, a crowd of 300 people had gathered. When the Riders entered the city, the crowd attacked the buses. One of the Riders, Jim Zwerg, was beaten to the ground. The crowd, armed with hammers, bats, and chains, then attacked the rest of the Riders.

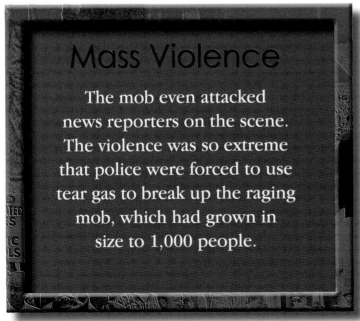

Mass Violence

The mob even attacked news reporters on the scene. The violence was so extreme that police were forced to use tear gas to break up the raging mob, which had grown in size to 1,000 people.

"My faith was never so strong as during that time. I knew I was doing what I should be doing." Jim Zwerg, member of the second Freedom Ride.

The Nation Takes Notice

Jim Zwerg's injuries from the Montgomery attack were so severe that he was hospitalized. News reporters interviewed the protester in his hospital bed, and the interview was shown on television across the United States. Jim's injuries and powerful words forced Americans everywhere to focus on the Freedom Riders' cause.

> "Segregation must be stopped. It must be broken down. Those of us on the Freedom Ride will continue. No matter what happens we are dedicated to this. We will take the beatings. We are willing to accept death. We are going to keep coming until we can ride anywhere in the South." Jim Zwerg.

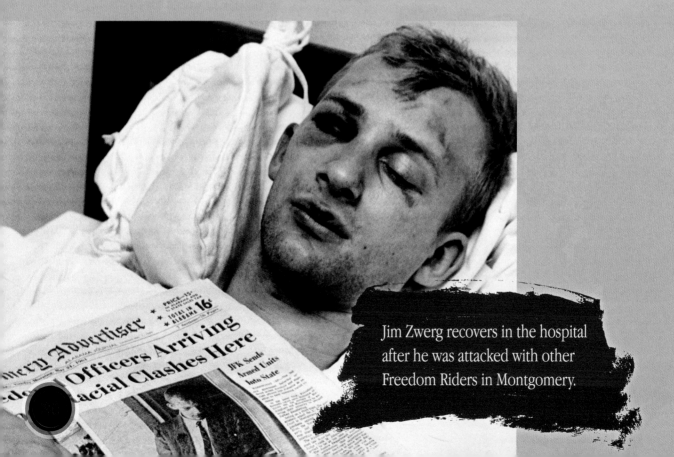

Jim Zwerg recovers in the hospital after he was attacked with other Freedom Riders in Montgomery.

The National Guard were ordered by the president to escort the Freedom Riders on the rest of their journey.

Safe Journey

On May 24, 27 Freedom Riders continued their journey from Montgomery to New Orleans. This time, the president had sent the National Guard to protect the Riders throughout their journey. The Greyhound buses were followed by 16 police cars, and soldiers were ordered to guard the Freedom Riders in Montgomery, Jackson, and New Orleans. When the two buses containing the Freedom Riders arrived in Jackson, no angry crowd awaited them.

Watched by the Nation

News reporters followed the Freedom Riders on their journey, and the protest was shown on television throughout the United States. Americans now knew what CORE was and what the organization was trying to achieve.

From Jackson to Jail

When the Freedom Riders finally arrived in Jackson, although their arrival was not met with violence, it was met with arrest. Local police arrested the Riders for using white restrooms and waiting rooms. The Riders spent their first night in Jackson in jail.

Freedom Riders sang freedom songs to lift their spirits after the brutal attacks in Montgomery.

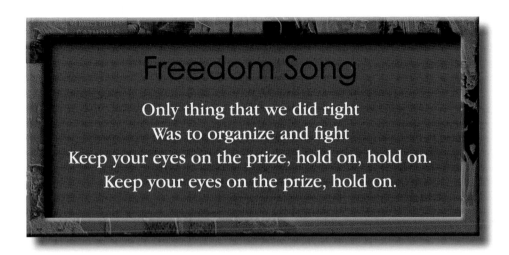

Freedom Song

Only thing that we did right
Was to organize and fight
Keep your eyes on the prize, hold on, hold on.
Keep your eyes on the prize, hold on.

To Prison and Plantation

The next day, the Freedom Riders were convicted of breaking the law. At their trial, they were accused of trespassing. The trial judge sentenced the Riders to 60 days in Mississippi's state prison. Many of the prisoners were moved from jail to jail, and some sent to the Parchman plantation. This was a jail in which prisoners were forced to work in plantation fields, all day long. Prisoners were sprayed with water hoses, hit with cattle prods, and had the mattresses on which they slept removed if they sang freedom songs.

Determined to Ride

Over the months that followed the Jackson trial, more than 1,000 Riders made a Freedom Ride to Jackson. The Riders understood that they might be imprisoned, but were determined to continue with their cause. Many Riders were arrested, and the jails and prisons in Jackson filled with protesters. Eventually, with the help of the NAACP, the prisoners had their convictions overturned.

More than four months after the first Freedom Ride had taken place, the Riders finally achieved victory. On September 22, 1961, the Interstate Commerce Commission passed a law. Transport stations were ordered to display notices stating that seating on public transport buses was to be "without regard to race, color, creed, or national origin."

> "We didn't give up. We didn't give in. We didn't despair. We kept the faith. We kept our eyes on the prize." John Lewis, Freedom Rider.

Testing the Rules

After the transport laws of 1961, CORE continued to carry out Freedom Rides to ensure laws were being upheld. The organization found that, finally, the law was being followed in 85 public transport stations

Children of all races across the United States can now sit side by side on public transport thanks to the Freedom Riders and their campaign.

The Greyhound bus station in Montgomery, Alabama, displays some of the famous photographs of the Freedom Rides.

in the South. Satisfied that its protest had been successful, in 1962, CORE announced that the battle against segregated seating had been won.

Safely and Freely

The first Freedom Ride undertaken by 13 brave men in 1961 had ensured the peaceful travel of thousands of African Americans through the southern states, in seating of their choice. These Freedom Riders had achieved their ultimate goal, complete desegregation in public transport services.

Riding into History

The Freedom Rides were part of a civil rights movement that swept across the United States in the 1960s. The movement led to important changes in African American history, such as the first African American judge, James B. Parsons, who was appointed by President Kennedy in 1961.

Peaceful Protests

Throughout the 1960s, peaceful, nonviolent protests won the American civil rights campaign. After the Freedom Rides had ended, many further protests were organized, which helped to bring an end to racial discrimination in the South.

"Their cause must be our cause too. Because it is not just Negroes but really it is all of us, who must overcome the crippling legacy of bigotry and injustice. And we shall overcome." President Johnson.

In the late 1950s, African American children started to attend the same schools as white children. School integration slowly took place all over the country.

Changes in Education

In 1954, a case at the US Supreme Court called *Brown v. Board of Education* ruled that segregation in schools was unfair. School desegregation took many years, and great determination by protesters, but slowly American schools began to integrate white American and African American students.

In 1963, members of the CORE organization took part in a protest that demanded racial equality. It was called the March on Washington for Jobs and Freedom.

Student Sit-Ins

After the success of the Montgomery bus boycott, African Americans recognized the impact that nonviolent protest could have. In 1960, in Greensboro, North Carolina, four students decided to sit down at a "whites only" lunch counter at their local Woolworth's department store. When they were refused service, the students continued to sit peacefully. As the number of students taking part in this silent protest grew, sit-ins took place at lunch counters all over the South. Eventually, storeowners were forced to desegregate their lunch counters, and both white and African Americans were served.

A Lasting Legacy

Pressure from civil rights protesters in the years that followed the Freedom Rides, encouraged President Kennedy to create a civil rights bill that would guarantee complete desegregation throughout the United States. However, the path to legal desegregation was not easy.

Birmingham Bomb

On September 15, 1963, a bomb exploded at the Sixteenth Street Baptist Church in Birmingham, Alabama. It killed four schoolgirls and injured many more. The nation was horrified at the death of innocent children. The church had been targeted because it was a meeting place used by Birmingham civil rights campaigners and civil rights leaders such as Martin Luther King Jr.

After the bombing at the Sixteenth Street Baptist Church, donations of more than $300,000 were received and used to restore the church building.

Today, thanks to the brave Freedom Riders' fight for equality, American children can enjoy a life of freedom.

Civil Rights Act

Two months after the Birmingham bombing, President Kennedy was shot dead in Texas. Kennedy had been in the process of putting his civil rights bill through government at the time of his death. Determined to see through the late president's bill, Kennedy's successor, President Lyndon B. Johnson, pushed through the bill. The Civil Rights Act was finally signed in July 1964, and the signing was attended by Martin Luther King Jr.

Facing Danger

The Act that changed the lives of African Americans forever would not have been possible were it not for the Freedom Riders. The brave men and women who had made their rides for freedom had faced bombings, beatings, and even death in their campaign for equality. It is because of their great sacrifices that African Americans are free today to make peaceful, safe journeys throughout the United States.

Glossary

bigotry (BIH-guh-tree) Intolerance of any group.

boycott (BOY-kot) To refuse to use.

campaign (kam-PAYN) A series of planned actions to reach a particular goal.

civil rights (SIH-vul RYTS) The rights given by a government to all its citizens.

conviction (kun-VIK-shun) When someone is found guilty of a crime.

desegregated (dee-SEH-gruh-gayt-ed) To stop the use of separate schools and facilities for people of different races.

escort (ES-kort) A group of people who travel with someone to protect them.

governor (GUH-vur-nur) A person in government. In the US governors are in charge of each state.

hospitalized (HOS-pih-tuh-lyzd) To be placed in hospital for medical treatment.

interstate (IN-tur-stayt) Passing through two or more states.

mob (MOB) A large crowd of angry people.

National Guard (NASH-nul GARD) A US military force maintained by each state, which can be called upon by either the state or federal government.

plantation (plan-TAY-shun) A large farm used for growing rubber, cotton, or other crops to sell.

protest (PROH-test) The formal action of a group of people who want something to change.

racial (RAY-shul) To do with a race of people.

reconciliation (reh-kun-sih-lee-AY-shun) The process of making something consistent. The Journey of Reconciliation hoped to make the laws on public buses consistent.

sacrifice (SA-kruh-fys) To give up something.

segregation (seh-gruh-GAY-shun) A system to keep white Americans and African Americans apart.

Supreme Court (suh-PREEM KORT) The highest court in the United States.

trespassing (TRES-pas-ing) Entering somewhere without permission.

volunteer (vah-lun-TEER) A person who offers to help.

will (WIL) A written statement about what a person wants to happen to them and their possessions after he or she has died.

Further Reading

Jeffrey, Gary. *Rosa Parks and the Montgomery Bus Boycott*. A Graphic History of the Civil Rights Movement. New York: Gareth Stevens Learning Library, 2012.

Mis, Melody S. *Meet Martin Luther King Jr.* Civil Rights Leaders. New York: PowerKids Press, 2008.

Skog, Jason. *The Civil Rights Act of 1964*. We the People: Modern America. Mankato, MN: Capstone Press, 2007.

Websites

Index